ORDER OF CHRISTIAN FUNERALS

Vigil Service
Evening Prayer

People's Edition

RITUAL DE EXEQUIAS CRISTIANAS

Vigilia por un difunto
Vísperas

Edición del Pueblo

LITURGICAL PRESS
Collegeville, Minnesota

www.litpress.org

Concordat cum originali
Monsignor James P. Moroney
Executive Director
USCCB Secretariat for the Liturgy

Cover design by/diseño de la cubierta por Ann Blattner

CONTENTS / ÍNDICE GENERAL

Vigil for the Deceased   4
Vigilia por un difunto   5

Evening Prayer for the Dead   18
Vísperas   19

Responsorial Psalms   34–39
Salmo Responsorial   59–62

Hymns   39–58
Himnos   62–71

Index/Índice   72

VIGIL FOR THE DECEASED

At the vigil the Christian community keeps watch with the family in prayer to the God of mercy and finds strength in Christ's presence. . . . In this time of loss the family and community turn to God's word as the source of faith and hope, as light and life in the face of darkness and death. Consoled by the redeeming word of God and by the abiding presence of Christ and his Spirit, the assembly at the vigil calls upon the Father of mercy to receive the deceased into the kingdom of light and peace.

—Order of Christian Funerals, 56

INTRODUCTORY RITES

GREETING

The minister greets those present, and all reply:

People:
And also with you.

OPENING SONG

The celebrations continues with song. A selection may be taken from nn. 1–54.

OPENING PRAYER

The minister invites those gathered to pray. All pause for silent prayer, and then the minister says a prayer aloud. At the conclusion, the assembly replies:

All:
Amen.

VIGILIA POR UN DIFUNTO

Durante la vigilia, la comunidad cristiana, junto con la familia, se mantiene en vela, orando al Dios de la misericordia y encuentra así la fortaleza que da la presencia de Cristo. Es la primera ocasión en medio de los ritos fúnebres para la proclamación solemne de la Palabra de Dios. En este momento de separación, la familia y la comunidad se vuelven a la Palabra de Dios como fuente de fe y esperanza, como luz y vida frente a la oscuridad y la muerte. La asamblea, consolada por la palabra de Cristo y su Espíritu, ruega al Padre misericordioso que reciba al difunto en el reino de luz y de paz. —Ritual de Exequias Cristianas, 56

RITOS INTRODUCTORIOS

SALUDO

El que preside saluda a los presentes, y todos responden:

Pueblo:

Y con tu espíritu.

CANTO DE ENTRADA

La celebración continúa con un canto. Se encuentra una selección de cantos en los nn. 1–54.

ORACIÓN DE ENTRADA

El que preside invita a orar a los que están reunidos. Todos hacen una pausa para orar en silencio, y después el que preside reza una oración en voz alta. Al final, los congregados responden:

Todos:

Amén.

LITURGY OF THE WORD

The proclamation of the word of God is the high point and central focus of the vigil. —Order of Christian Funerals, 59

The purpose of the readings at the vigil is to proclaim the paschal mystery, teach remembrance of the dead, convey the hope of being gathered together in God's kingdom, and encourage the witness of Christian life. —Order of Christian Funerals, 60

FIRST READING

A reader proclaims the first reading, ending with:

Reader:

The Word of the Lord.

All:

Thanks be to God.

RESPONSORIAL PSALM *(sung)*

The responsorial psalm enables the community to respond in faith to the reading and to express its grief and its praise of God.
—Order of Christian Funerals, 60

Suitable responsorial settings are available. See nn. 1–12 and 36–42. Spoken versions are found on pages 12–17.

GOSPEL

The gospel reading is then proclaimed.

Leader:

A reading from the holy gospel according to N.

All:

Glory to you, Lord.

The gospel concludes:

Leader:

The Gospel of the Lord.

All:

Praise to you, Lord Jesus Christ.

HOMILY

LITURGIA DE LA PALABRA

La proclamación de la Palabra de Dios es el punto culminante y eje central de la vigilia. —Ritual de Exequias Cristianas, 59

Las lecturas en la vigilia tienen la intención de proclamar el misterio pascual, de enseñar la piedad para con los difuntos, de alimentar la esperanza del reencuentro en el reino de Dios y de exhortar al testimonio de la vida cristiana. —Ritual de Exequias Cristianas, 60

PRIMERA LECTURA

Un lector proclama la primera lectura, y al final dice:

Lector:

Palabra de Dios.

Todos:

Te alabamos, Señor.

SALMO RESPONSORIAL *(cantado)*

El salmo responsorial permite a la comunidad responder con fe a la lectura; y permite también expresar su dolor y su alabanza a Dios.
—Ritual de Exequias Cristianas, 60

En los nn. 1–12 y 36–42 se encuentran versiones adecuadas de salmos responsoriales. Se pueden encontrar versiones recitadas en las páginas 12–17.

EVANGELIO

Después se proclama el Evangelio.

El que preside:

Lectura del santo Evangelio según San N.

Todos:

Gloria a tí, Señor.

El Evangelio concluye.

El que preside:

El Evangelio del Señor.

Todos:

Gloria a tí, Señor Jesúcristo.

HOMILÍA

PRAYER OF INTERCESSION

In the prayer of intercession the community calls upon God to comfort the mourners and to show mercy to the deceased.
—Order of Christian Funerals, 62

LITANY

The minister leads those present in the following litany. Each petition concludes:

Assisting minister:

Lord, have mercy.

All:

Lord, have mercy.

Or:

Assisting minister:

We pray to the Lord.

All:

We pray to the Lord.

Or:

Assisting minister:

Lord, in your mercy:

All:

Hear our prayer.

THE LORD'S PRAYER

The minister invites those present to pray the Lord's Prayer.

All:

Our Father . . .

CONCLUDING PRAYER

All:

Amen.

PRECES

En las preces la comunidad pide a Dios que consuele a los dolientes y que muestre su misericordia para con el difunto.

—Ritual de Exequias Cristianas, 62

Letanía

El que preside guía a los presentes en la siguiente letanía. Cada petición concluye con:

El asistente:
Señor, ten piedad.

Todos:
Señor, ten piedad.

O:

El asistente:
Oremos al Señor.

Todos:
Señor, oye nuestra oración.

O:

El asistente:
Señor, en tu misericordia:

Todos:
Oye nuestra oración.

Padrenuestro

El que preside invita a los presentes a rezar el Padrenuestro.

Todos:
Padre nuestro . . .

Oración Final

Todos:
Amén.

After the minister prays the concluding prayer, a member of the family or a friend of the deceased may speak in remembrance of the deceased.

CONCLUDING RITE

BLESSING

The minister says:

Blessed are those who have died in the Lord;
let them rest from their labors for their good deeds go with them.

A gesture, for example, signing the forehead of the deceased with the sign of the cross, may accompany the following words.

Leader:

Eternal rest grant unto him/her, O Lord.

All:

And let the perpetual light shine upon him/her.

Leader:

May he/she rest in peace.

All:

Amen.

Leader:

May his/her soul and the souls of all the faithful departed, through the mercy of God, rest in peace.

All:

Amen.

The minister invokes an appropriate blessing to which all reply:

All:

Amen.

The vigil may conclude with a song or a few moments of silent prayer or both.

The following spoken responsorial psalms may be used. Other responsorial psalms may be found either in the Lectionary, no 791, or in the *Order of Christian Funerals.*

Después de la oración final, un familiar o un amigo de la familia puede pronunciar unas palabras en recuerdo del difunto.

RITO DE CONCLUSIÓN

BENDICIÓN

El que preside dice:

Dichosos los que mueren en el Señor; que descansen ya de sus fatigas, pues sus obras los acompañan.

Las palabras que siguen pueden ir acompañadas de un gesto, por ejemplo, el de hacer la señal de la cruz en la frente del difunto.

El que preside:

Concédele, Señor, el descanso eterno.

Todos:

Y brille para él (ella) la luz perpetua.

El que preside:

Descanse en paz.

Todos:

Amén.

El que preside:

El alma de N. y las almas de todos los fieles difuntos, por la misericordia de Dios, descansen en paz.

Todos:

Amén.

El que preside invoca una bendición apropiada a la que todos responden:

Todos:

Amén.

La vigilia puede concluir con un canto o con un breve tiempo de oración en silencio, o con ambos.

Se pueden usar los siguientes salmos responsoriales recitados. Se pueden encontrar otros salmos responsoriales en el Leccionario, num. 791, o en el *Ritual de Exequias Cristianas*.

℟. (1a) **The Lord is my light and my salvation.**
or: (13) **I believe that I shall see the good things of the Lord in the land of the living.**

The LORD is my light and my salvation;
  whom should I fear?
The LORD is my life's refuge;
  of whom should I be afraid?

℟. **The Lord is my light and my salvation.**
or: **I believe that I shall see the good things of the Lord in the land of the living.**

One thing I ask of the LORD;
  this I seek:
To dwell in the house of the LORD
  all the days of my life,
That I may gaze on the loveliness of the LORD
  and contemplate his temple.

℟. **The Lord is my light and my salvation.**
or: **I believe that I shall see the good things of the Lord in the land of the living.**

Hear, O LORD, the sound of my call;
  have pity on me, and answer me.
Your presence, O LORD, I seek.
  Hide not your face from me.

℟. **The Lord is my light and my salvation.**
or: **I believe that I shall see the good things of the Lord in the land of the living.**

I believe that I shall see the bounty of the LORD
  in the land of the living.
Wait for the LORD with courage;
  be stouthearted, and wait for the LORD.

R⁊. **El Señor es mi luz y mi salvación.**
O bien: **Espero gozar de la dicha del Señor en el país de la vida.**

El Señor es mi luz y mi salvación,
¿a quién temeré?
El Señor es la defensa de mi vida,
¿quién me hará temblar?

R⁊. **El Señor es mi luz y mi salvación.**
O bien: **Espero gozar de la dicha del Señor en el país de la vida.**

Una cosa pido al Señor,
eso buscaré:
habitar en la casa del Señor
por los días de mi vida;
gozar de la dulzura del Señor,
contemplando su templo.

R⁊. **El Señor es mi luz y mi salvación.**
O bien: **Espero gozar de la dicha del Señor en el país de la vida.**

Escúchame, Señor, que te llamo;
ten piedad, respóndeme.
Tu rostro buscaré, Señor,
no me escondas tu rostro.

R⁊. **El Señor es mi luz y mi salvación.**
O bien: **Espero gozar de la dicha del Señor en el país de la vida.**

Espero gozar de la dicha del Señor
en el país de la vida.
Espera en el Señor, sé valiente,
ten ánimo, espera en el Señor.

R⁊. **El Señor es mi luz y mi salvación.**
O bien: **Espero gozar de la dicha del Señor en el país de la vida.**

℟. (1) **Out of the depths, I cry to you, Lord.**
or: (see 50) **I hope in the Lord, I trust in his word.**

Out of the depths I cry to you, O LORD;
  LORD, hear my voice!
Let your ears be attentive
  to my voice in supplication.

℟. **Out of the depths, I cry to you, Lord.**
or: **I hope in the Lord, I trust in his word.**

If you, O LORD, mark iniquities,
  LORD, who can stand?
But with you is forgiveness,
  that you may be revered.

℟. **Out of the depths, I cry to you, Lord.**
or: **I hope in the Lord, I trust in his word.**

I trust in the LORD;
  my soul trusts in his word.
My soul waits for the LORD
  more than the sentinels wait for the dawn.

℟. **Out of the depths, I cry to you, Lord.**
or: **I hope in the Lord, I trust in his word.**

More than the sentinels wait for the dawn,
  let Israel wait for the LORD,
For with the LORD is kindness
  and with him is plenteous redemption.

℟. **Out of the depths, I cry to you, Lord.**
or: **I hope in the Lord, I trust in his word.**

And he will redeem Israel
  from all their iniquities.

℟. **Out of the depths, I cry to you, Lord.**
or: **I hope in the Lord, I trust in his word.**

R℣. **Desde lo hondo a ti grito, Señor.**
O bien: **Espero en el Señor, espero en su palabra.**

Desde lo hondo a ti grito, Señor;
Señor, escucha mi voz;
estén tus oídos atentos
a la voz de mi súplica.

R℣. **Desde lo hondo a ti grito, Señor.**
O bien: **Espero en el Señor, espero en su palabra.**

Si llevas cuenta de los delitos, Señor,
¿quién podrá resistir?
Pero de ti procede el perdón,
y así infundes respeto.

R℣. **Desde lo hondo a ti grito, Señor.**
O bien: **Espero en el Señor, espero en su palabra.**

Mi alma espera en el Señor,
espera en su palabra;
mi alma aguarda al Señor,
más que el centinela la aurora.

R℣. **Desde lo hondo a ti grito, Señor.**
O bien: **Espero en el Señor, espero en su palabra.**

Aguarde Israel al Señor,
como el centinela la aurora;
porque del Señor viene la misericordia,
la redención copiosa.

R℣. **Desde lo hondo a ti grito, Señor.**
O bien: **Espero en el Señor, espero en su palabra.**

Y él redimirá a Israel
de todos sus delitos.

R℣. **Desde lo hondo a ti grito, Señor.**
O bien: **Espero en el Señor, espero en su palabra.**

℟. (9) **I will walk in the presence of the Lord in the land of the living.**
or: **Alleluia.**

Gracious is the LORD and just;
yes, our God is merciful.

℟. **I will walk in the presence of the Lord in the land of the living.**
or: **Alleluia.**

The LORD keeps the little ones;
I was brought low, and he saved me.

℟. **I will walk in the presence of the Lord in the land of the living.**
or: **Alleluia.**

I believed, even when I said,
"I am greatly afflicted";
I said in my alarm,
"No man is dependable."

℟. **I will walk in the presence of the Lord in the land of the living.**
or: **Alleluia.**

Precious in the eyes of the LORD
is the death of his faithful ones.
O LORD, I am your servant,
you have loosed my bonds.

℟. **I will walk in the presence of the Lord in the land of the living.**
or: **Alleluia.**

3   Salmo 114 (116), 5-6; y 115 (116), 10-11. 15-16ac

℞. **Caminaré en presencia del Señor**
en el país de la vida.
O bien: **Aleluya.**

El Señor es benigno y justo,
nuestro Dios es compasivo;
el Señor guarda a los sencillos:
estando yo sin fuerzas, me salvó.

℞. **Caminaré en presencia del Señor**
en el país de la vida.
O bien: **Aleluya.**

Tenía fe, aun cuando dije:
"¡Qué desgraciado soy!"
Yo decía en mi apuro:
"Los hombres son unos mentirosos."

℞. **Caminaré en presencia del Señor**
en el país de la vida.
O bien: **Aleluya.**

Mucho le cuesta al Señor
la muerte de sus fieles.
Señor, yo soy tu siervo:
rompiste mis cadenas.

℞. **Caminaré en presencia del Señor**
en el país de la vida.
O bien: **Aleluya.**

EVENING PRAYER FOR THE DEAD

In the celebration of the office for the dead, members of the Christian community gather to offer praise and thanks for God, especially for the gifts of redemption and resurrection, to intercede for the dead, and to find strength in Christ's victory over death. When the community celebrates the hours, Christ the Mediator and High Priest is truly present through his Spirit in the gathered assembly, in the proclamation of God's word, and in the prayer and song of the Church. —Order of Christian Funerals, 349

. . . Through evening prayer from the office for the dead the community gives thanks to God for the gift of life received by the deceased and praises the Father for the redemption brought about by the sacrifice of his Son, who is the joy-giving light and the true source of hope. —Order of Christian Funerals, 351

INTRODUCTORY VERSE

All stand and make the sign of the cross as the minister says:

Minister:

God, come to my assistance.

All:

Lord, make haste to help me.

Minister:

Glory to the Father, and to the Son, and to the Holy Spirit:

All:

As it was in the beginning, is now, and will be for ever. Amen [outside Lent: Alleluia].

HYMN

The celebration continues with a hymn. See nn. 1–54 or another suitable hymn.

VÍSPERAS

En la celebración del oficio de difuntos, la comunidad cristiana se reúne para alabar y agradecer a Dios, especialmente por los dones de la redención y de la resurrección; para interceder por los muertos y para hallar fortaleza en el triunfo de Cristo sobre la muerte. Cuando la comunidad celebra la liturgia de las horas, Cristo, Mediador y Sumo Sacerdote, está realmente presente por su Espíritu en la asamblea congregada, en la Palabra de Dios que se proclama, y en la oración y canto de la Iglesia.

—Ritual de Exequias Cristianas, 349

. . . Por Vísperas del oficio de difuntos a la comunidad agradece a Dios por el don de la vida que recibió el difunto y glorifica al Padre por la redención que nos ha traído el sacrificio de su Hijo, luz gozosa, y fuente verdadera de toda esperanza.

—Ritual de Exequias Cristianas, 351

INVOCACIÓN INICIAL

Todos se ponen de pie y hacen la señal de la cruz mientras el que preside dice:

El que preside:
Dios mío, ven en mi auxilio.

Todos:
Señor, date prisa en socorrerme.

El que preside:
Gloria al Padre, y al Hijo, y al Espíritu Santo:

Todos:
Como era en el principio, ahora y siempre, por los siglos de los siglos. Amén [fuera del tiempo cuaresmal: Aleluya].

HIMNO

La celebración continúa con uno de los himnos que se encuentran en los nn. 1–54 o con otro himno apropiado.

PSALMODY

During the psalms and canticle,[1] all may sit or stand, according to custom.

The psalms and canticles should be sung. If they cannot be sung, they should be spoken slowly and reflectively.

A period of silence follows each psalm.

First Psalm—The cantor sings the antiphon and all repeat it. The cantor then sings the stanza of the psalm and all repeat the antiphon after each stanza.

Acc. p. 122

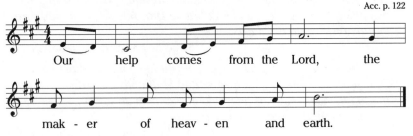

Our help comes from the Lord, the mak - er of heav - en and earth.

Psalm 121

Cantor:

I lift up my eyes to the mountains:
from where shall come my help?
My help shall come from the Lord
who made heaven and earth. *Ant.*

Cantor:

May he never allow you to stumble!
Let him sleep not, your guard.
No, he sleeps not nor slumbers,
Israel's guard. *Ant.*

Cantor:

The Lord is your guard and your shade;
at your right side he stands.
By day the sun shall not smite you
nor the moon in the night. *Ant.*

1. The method for singing each psalm and canticle as presented here is one way that may be used; other ways may also be used.

SALMODIA

Mientras se entonen los salmos y el cántico[1] todos pueden estar sentados o permanecer de pie, según la costumbre local.

Los salmos y cánticos se deben cantar. Si no pueden ser cantados, se deben recitar lenta y reflexivamente.

Un período de silencio sigue a cada salmo.

Primer Salmo—El solista canta la antífona y todos la repiten. Después el solista canta las estrofas del salmo y todos repiten la antífona después de cada estrofa.

ESTRIBILLO — *Cantor/Todos* — Acc. p. 174

El au - xi - lio me vie - ne del Se - ñor
que hi - zo el cie - lo_y la tie - rra.

Salmo 120 (121)

Solista:

Levanto mis ojos a los montes:
¿de dónde me vendrá el auxilio?
El auxilio me viene del Señor,
que hizo el cielo y la tierra. *Ant.*

Solista:

No permitirá que resbale tu pie,
tu guardián no duerme;
no duerme ni reposa
el guardián de Israel. *Ant.*

Solista:

El Señor te guarda a su sombra,
está a tu derecha;
de día el sol no te hará daño,
ni la luna de noche. *Ant.*

1. Véase *Misal Romano*, Instrucción General para el Uso del Misal Romano, núm. 336. El método que aquí se presenta para cantar cada salmo y cántico es sólo uno de los que se pueden utilizar; otros métodos también pueden utilizarse.

21

Cantor:

The Lord will guard you from evil,
he will guard your soul.
The Lord will guard your going and coming
both now and forever. *Ant.*

All:

Glory to the Father, and to the Son,
and to the Holy Spirit:
as it was in the beginning, is now,
and will be for ever. Amen. *Ant.*

(A period of silence)

Second Psalm—The cantor sings the antiphon and all repeat it. Two
groups alternate singing the stanzas of the psalm; the last stanza, the
doxology, is sung by all. The antiphon may be repeated by all after the
doxology.

Boldface type signals the change of pitch for the flex (+), the middle
(*), and the cadence.

RESPONSE   Acc. p. 181

If you kept a re-cord of our sins, O Lord, who could es-

cape your con-dem-na-tion?

Psalm 130

Group 1:

Out of the depths I cry to you, **O** Lord;*
Lord, **hear** my voice!
O let your ears be **at**tentive*
to the voice **of** my pleading. *Ant.*

Group 2:

If you, O Lord, should mark **our** guilt,*
Lord, who **would** survive?
But with you is found **for**giveness:*
for this **we** revere you. *Ant.*

Solista:

El Señor te guarda de todo mal,
él guarda tu alma;
el Señor guarda tus entradas y salidas,
ahora y por siempre. *Ant.*

Todos:

Gloria al Padre, y al Hijo, y al Espíritu Santo:
como era en el principio, ahora y siempre,
por los siglos de los siglos. Amén. *Ant.*

(Un período de silencio)

Segundo Salmo—El solista canta la antífona y todos la repiten. Dos
grupos se turnan para cantar las estrofas del salmo; todos cantan la
última estrofa (la doxología). Después de la doxología, todos pueden
repetir la antífona.

Las letras en negrita señalan el cambio de tono para el flex (+), el centro (*), y la cadencia.

Acc. p. 181

RESPUESTA

Si lle - vas cuen-ta de los de - li - tos, Se - ñor, ¿qui-

én po - drá re - sis - tir?

Salmo 129 (130)

Grupo 1:

Desde lo hondo a ti grito, **Señor;***
Señor, escu**cha** mi voz;
estén tus oídos **a**tentos*
a la voz **de** mi súplica. *Ant.*

Grupo 2:

Si llevas cuenta de los delitos, **Señor,***
¿quién podrá **re**sistir?
Pero de ti procede el **per**dón,*
y así infun**des** respeto. *Ant.*

Group 1:

My soul is waiting for **the** Lord,*
I count **on** his word.
My soul is longing for **the** Lord*
more than watch**man** for daybreak.
Let the watchman count **on** daybreak*
and Israel **on** the Lord. *Ant.*

Group 2:

Because with the Lord there **is** mercy*
and fullness **of** redemption,
Israel indeed he will **re**deem*
from all **its** iniquity. *Ant.*

All:

Glory to the Father, and to **the** Son,*
and to the **Ho**ly Spirit:
as it was in the **begin**ning,*
is now, and will be for **ev**er. Amen. *Ant.*

Canticle—The cantor sings the antiphon and all repeat it; the cantor then sings the stanzas of the canticle and all repeat the antiphon after each stanza.

Boldface type signals the change of pitch for the flex (+), the middle (*), and the cadence.

Acc. p. 23

Canticle: Philippians 2:6-11

Ant.   As the Father raises the dead and gives **them** life, *
so the Son gives life to **whom** he wills.

Cantor:

Though he was in the form of **God,**+
he did not deem equality **with** God*
something **to** be grasped at. *Ant.*

Cantor:

Rather, he emptied him**self**+
and took the form of **a** slave,*
being born in the like**ness** of men. *Ant.*

24

Grupo 1:

Mi alma espera en el **Se**ñor,*
espera en **su** palabra;
mi alma aguarda al **Se**ñor,*
más que el centinela **la** aurora. *Ant.*

Grupo 2:

Aguarde Israel al **Se**ñor,*
como el centinela **la** aurora;
porque del Señor viene la mise**ri**cordia,*
la redención **co**piosa;
y él redimirá **a** Israel*
de todos **sus** delitos. *Ant.*

Todos:

Gloria al Padre, y **al** Hijo,*
y al Espí**ri**tu Santo:
como era en el principio, ahora y **si**empre,*
por los siglos de los si**glos**. Amén. *Ant.*

Cántico—El solista canta la antífona y todos la repiten; después canta
las estrofas del cántico y todos repiten la antífona después de cada
estrofa.

Las letras en negrita señalan el cambio de tono para el flex (+), el centro (*), y la cadencia.

Acc. p. 24

Cántico: Filipenses 2, 6-11

Ant. Lo mismo que el Padre resucita a los muertos y les **da** vida,*
así también el Hijo da vida a **los** que quiere.

Solista:

Cristo, a pesar de su condición di**vi**na,*
no hizo alarde de su categoría **de** Dios. *Ant.*

Solista:

Al contrario, se despojó de su **ran**go+
y tomó la condición de **es**clavo,*
pasando por u**no** de tantos. *Ant.*

Cantor:

He was known to be of human **es**tate,*
  and it was thus that he hum**bled** himself,
  obediently accepting ev**en** death,*
  death **on** a cross! *Ant.*

Cantor:

Because **of** this,*
  God highly exa**lt**ed him
  and bestowed on him **the** name*
  above every **o**ther name, *Ant.*

Cantor:

So that at Je**sus'** name*
  every **knee** must bend
  in the heavens, on **the** earth,*
  and und**er** the earth,
  and every tongue pro**claim**+
  to the glory of God **the** Father:*
  JESUS **CHRIST** IS LORD! *Ant.*

Cantor:

Glory to the Father, and to **the** Son,*
and to the **Ho**ly Spirit:
as it was in the **be**ginning,*
is now, and will be for ev**er.** Amen. *Ant.*

READING

A reading from Scripture is proclaimed by the reader.

A period of silence may be observed; this may be followed by a brief homily.

RESPONSORY

One of the following responsories is then said:

A Cantor or reader:

In you, Lord, is our hope. We shall never hope in vain.

All:

In you, Lord, is our hope. We shall never hope in vain.

Cantor or reader:

We shall be glad and rejoice in your mercy.

All:

We shall never hope in vain.

Solista:

Y así, actuando como un hombre cual**quier**a,+
se rebajó hasta someterse incluso a **la** muerte,*
y una muer**te** de cruz. *Ant.*

Solista:

Por **eso**+
Dios lo levantó so**bre** todo*
y le concedió el "Nombre-sobre-**to**do-nombre." *Ant.*

Solista:

De modo que al nombre de Jesús toda rodilla **se** doble*
en el cielo, en la tierra, en **el** abismo,
y toda lengua **pro**clame:*
Jesucristo es Señor, para gloria de **Di**os Padre. *Ant.*

Solista:

Gloria al Padre, y al Hijo, y al Espíri**tu** Santo:+
como era en el principio, ahora **y** siempre,*
por los siglos de los si**glos**. Amén. *Ant.*

Lectura

El lector proclama una lectura de la Sagrada Escritura.

Se puede guardar un período de silencio; a éste le puede seguir por una breve homilía.

Responsorio

Después se recita uno de los siguientes responsorios.

A   Solista o lector:

A ti, Señor, me acojo. No quede nunca yo defraudado.

Todos:

A ti, Señor, me acojo. No quede nunca yo defraudado.

Solista o lector:

Tu misericordia sea mi gozo y mi alegría.

Todos:

No quede nunca yo defraudado.

27

Cantor or reader:

Glory to the Father, and to the Son, and to the Holy Spirit.

All:

In you, Lord, is our hope. We shall never hope in vain.

B Cantor or reader:

Lord, in your steadfast love, give them eternal rest.

All:

Lord, in your steadfast love, give them eternal rest.

Cantor or reader:

You will come to judge the living and the dead.

All:

Give them eternal rest.

Cantor or reader:

Glory to the Father, and to the Son, and to the Holy Spirit.

All:

Lord, in your steadfast love, give them eternal rest.

CANTICLE OF MARY

If evening prayer is celebrated in the church, the altar may be in-
censed during the canticle, then the minister and the congregation.
All stand as one of the following antiphons is sung by the cantor and
then repeated by all.

Boldface type signals the change of pitch for the flex (+), the middle
(*), and the cadence.

Acc. p. 22

Outside the Easter Season:

Ant.　All that the Father gives me will come **to** me,*
　　　and whoever comes to me I shall not **turn** away.

Or:

During the Easter Season:

Ant.　Our crucified and ri**sen** Lord*
　　　has redeemed us, **al**leluia.

Gloria al Padre, y al Hijo, y al Espíritu Santo.

Todos:

A ti, Señor, me acojo. No quede nunca yo defraudado.

B Solista o lector:

En tu misericordia, Señor, concédeles el descanso.

Todos:

En tu misericordia, Señor, concédeles el descanso.

Solista o lector:

Tú que has de venir a juzgar a vivos y muertos.

Todos:

Concédeles el descanso.

Solista o lector:

Gloria al Padre, y al Hijo, y al Espíritu Santo.

Todos:

En tu misericordia, Señor, concédeles el descanso.

CÁNTICO DE MARÍA

Si las Vísperas se celebran en la iglesia, durante el cántico se inciensa el altar, y después al que preside y a la congregación. Todos se ponen de pie mientras el solista canta una de las siguientes antífonas, que todos repetirán después.

Las letras en negrita señalan el cambio de tono para el flex (+), el centro (*), y la cadencia.

Acc. p. 25

Fuera del tiempo Pascual:

Ant.   Todos los que el Padre me ha entregado vendrán **a** mí;*
y al que venga a mí no lo **echa**ré fuera.

O bien:

Durante el tiempo Pascual:

Ant.   El **Cru**cificado resucitó de entre los muertos y nos redi**mió**.*
Aleluya.

All then make the sign of the cross as the canticle begins. The stanzas of the canticle are sung by all and the antiphon is repeated after the last stanza.

All:

Luke 1:46-55

My soul proclaims the greatness of the **Lord,**+
my spirit rejoices in God **my** Savior;*
for he has looked with favor on his **low**ly servant.

From this day all generations will call me **blessed:**+
the Almighty has done great things **for** me,*
and holy **is** his Name.

He has mercy on those **who** fear him*
in every **gen**eration.

He has shown the strength of **his** arm,*
he has scattered the proud in **their** conceit.

He has cast down the mighty from **their** thrones,*
and has lifted **up** the lowly.

He has filled the hungry **with** good things,*
and the rich he has sent **a**way empty.

He has come to the help of his ser**vant** Israel*
for he has remembered his prom**ise** of mercy,
the promise he made to **our** fathers,*
to Abraham and his child**ren** for ever.

Glory to the Father, and to **the** Son,*
and to the **Ho**ly Spirit:
as it was in the **be**ginning,*
is now, and will be fore**ver.** Amen.

The antiphon is repeated.

Outside the Easter Season:

Ant.　All that the Father gives me will come **to** me,*
　　　and whoever comes to me I shall not **turn** away.

Or:

During the Easter Season:

Ant.　Our crucified and ri**sen** Lord*
　　　has redeemed us, **al**leluia.

30

Después todos hacen la señal de la cruz al comenzar el cántico. Todos cantan las estrofas y después de la última estrofa se repite la antífona.

Todos:

Lucas 1, 46-55

Proclama mi alma la grandeza del Señor,+
se alegra mi espíritu en Dios, mi salvador;*
porque ha mirado la humillación de su esclava.

Desde ahora me felicitarán todas las generaciones,*
porque el Poderoso ha hecho obras grandes por mí:
su nombre es santo,+
y su misericordia llega a sus fieles*
de generación en generación.

Él hace proezas con su brazo:*
dispersa a los soberbios de corazón,
derriba del trono a los poderosos*
y enaltece a los humildes,
a los hambrientos los colma de bienes*
y a los ricos los despide vacíos.

Auxilia a Israel, su siervo,*
acordándose de la misericordia
—como lo había prometido a nuestros padres—*
en favor de Abrahán y su descendencia por siempre.

Gloria al Padre, y al Hijo, y al Espíritu Santo:+
como era en el principio, ahora y siempre,*
por los siglos de los siglos. Amén.

La antífona se repite.

Fuera del tiempo Pascual:

Ant.   Todos los que el Padre me ha entregado vendrán a mí; y*
al que venga a mí no lo echaré fuera.

O bien:

Durante el tiempo Pascual:

Ant.   El Crucificado resucitó de entre los muertos y nos redimió.*
Aleluya.

31

All respond:

Lord, you are our life and resurrection.

THE LORD'S PRAYER

CONCLUDING PRAYER

All:

Amen.

After the minister prays the concluding prayer, a member of the family or a friend of the deceased may speak in remembrance of the deceased.

DISMISSAL

The minister then blesses the people:

A   A minister who is a priest or deacon says the following or another form of blessing, as at Mass.

The Lord be with you.

All:

And also with you.

A blessing is given, to which all reply:

All:

Amen.

B   A lay minister invokes God's blessing and signs himself or herself with the sign of the cross, saying:

**May the Lord bless us,
protect us from all evil
and bring us to everlasting life.**

All:

Amen.

Minister:

Go in peace.

All:

Thanks be to God.

The vigil may conclude with a song or a few moments of silent prayer or both.

PRECES

Todos responden:
Tú, Señor, eres nuestra vida y nuestra resurrección.

PADRENUESTRO

ORACIÓN FINAL

Todos:
Amén.

Después de la oración final, un familiar o un amigo de la familia puede pronunciar unas palabras en recuerdo del difunto.

DESPEDIDA

Después el que preside bendice al pueblo.

A   Si el que preside es sacerdote o un diácono, se utiliza la siguente, u otra, bendición como en la Misa:

El Señor esté con ustedes.

Todos:
Y con tu espíritu.

Se da la bendición, a la que todos responden:

Todos:
Amén.

B   Si el que preside es un laico, invoca la bendición de Dios y se persigna con la señal de la cruz, mientras dice:

El Señor nos bendiga,
nos guarde de todo mal
y nos lleve a la vida eterna.

℞. **Amén.**

El que preside:
Pueden ir en paz.

Todos:
Demos gracias a Dios.

La vigilia puede concluir con una canción, con un breve período de oración en silencio, o con ambos.

1. Psalm 16: Shelter Me, O God

Acc. p. 100

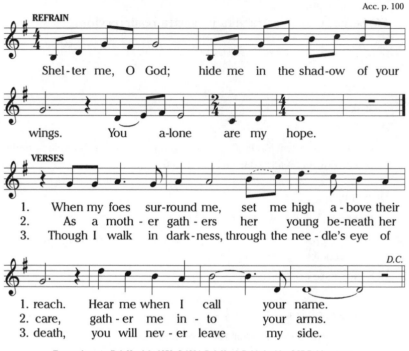

REFRAIN

Shel-ter me, O God; hide me in the shad-ow of your wings. You a-lone are my hope.

VERSES

1. When my foes sur-round me, set me high a-bove their
2. As a moth-er gath-ers her young be-neath her
3. Though I walk in dark-ness, through the nee-dle's eye of

D.C.

1. reach. Hear me when I call your name.
2. care, gath-er me in-to your arms.
3. death, you will nev-er leave my side.

2. Psalm 23: Shepherd Me, O God

Acc. p. 102

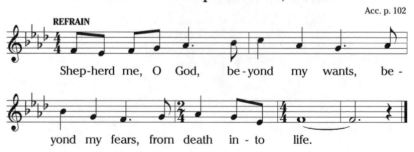

REFRAIN

Shep-herd me, O God, be-yond my wants, be-yond my fears, from death in-to life.

3. Psalm 23: The Lord Is My Shepherd

Acc. p. 106

The Lord is my shep - herd, noth - ing shall I want:

he leads me by safe paths, noth - ing shall I fear.

Text: The Grail, England, © 1963.
Music: A. Gregory Murray, O.S.B., © 1963, The Grail, England. GIA Publications, Inc., North American agent.

4. Psalm 27: The Lord Is My Light

Acc. p. 108

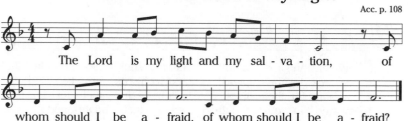

The Lord is my light and my sal - va - tion, of

whom should I be a - fraid, of whom should I be a - fraid?

Text and music: David Haas, b. 1957, © 1983, GIA Publications, Inc.

5. Psalm 27: The Lord Is My Light

Acc. p. 110

The Lord is my light and my sal - va - tion; the

Lord is my light and my sal - va - tion.

Text: *Lectionary for Mass,* © 1969, 1981, 1997, ICEL. All rights reserved. Used with permission.
Music: Christopher Willcock, S.J. © 1976, Christopher Willcock, S.J. Published by OCP Publications, Inc.

6. Psalm 42/43: Like the Deer That Longs

Acc. p. 114

Like the deer that longs for run - ning streams, my

soul longs for you my God.

Text: *Lectionary for Mass,* © 1969, 1981, 1997, ICEL. All rights reserved. Used with permission.
Music: Jay F. Hunstiger, b. 1950, © 1984, Jay F. Hunstiger, administered by Liturgical Press, Collegeville, MN.

7. Psalm 34: The Cry of the Poor

Acc. p. 112

REFRAIN

The Lord hears the cry of the poor. Bless-ed be the Lord.

VERSES

1. I will bless the Lord at all times, with praise
2. Let the low-ly hear and be glad: the Lord
3. Ev-'ry spir-it crushed, God will save; will be
4. We pro-claim your great-ness, O God, your praise

1. ev-er in my mouth. Let my soul glo-ry in the
2. lis-tens to their pleas; and to hearts bro-ken, God is
3. ran-som for their lives; will be safe shel-ter for their
4. ev-er in our mouth; ev-'ry face bright-ened in your

D.C.

1. Lord, who will hear the cry of the poor.
2. near, who will hear the cry of the poor.
3. fears, and will hear the cry of the poor.
4. light, for you hear the cry of the poor.

8. Psalm 63: My Soul Is Thirsting

Acc. p. 116

My soul is thir-sting for you, O Lord my God.

9. Psalm 42: Like the Deer That Yearns

Acc. p. 113

REFRAIN

My soul is thirst - ing for the Lord:

when shall I see him face to face?

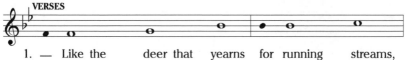

VERSES

1. — Like the deer that yearns for running streams,
2. My soul is thirsting for God, the God of my life;
3. My tears have be-come my bread, by night, by day,
4. By day the Lord will send his loving kindness;

1. — so my soul is yearning for you, my God.
2. — when can I enter and see the face of God?
3. as I hear it said all daylong; — "Where is your God?"
4. by night I will sing to him, praise the God of my life.

10. Psalm 63: Your Love Is Finer Than Life

Acc. p. 118

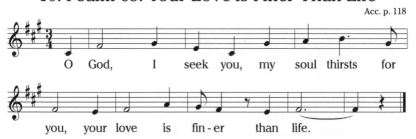

O God, I seek you, my soul thirsts for

you, your love is fin - er than life.

11. Psalm 139: You Are Near

Acc. p. 124

REFRAIN

Yah-weh, I know you are near, stand-ing al - ways at my side. You guard me from the foe, and you lead me in ways e - ver - last-ing.

VERSES

1. Lord, you have searched my heart, and you know when I sit and when I stand. Your hand is up - on me pro-tect-ing me from death, keep-ing me from harm.

2. Where can I run from your love?
   If I climb to the heavens you are there;
   if I fly to the sunrise or sail beyond the sea,
   still I'd find you there.

3. You know my heart and its ways,
   you who formed me before I was born,
   in secret of darkness before I saw the sun,
   in my mother's womb.

4. Marvelous to me are your works;
   how profound are your thoughts, my Lord.
   Even if I could count them, they number as the stars,
   you would still be there.

12. Psalm 84: How Lovely Is Your Dwelling Place

Acc. p. 120

How love-ly is your dwell-ing place, O Lord of hosts.

Text: Psalm 84:2, The Grail.
Music: A. Gregory Murray, O.S.B., © 1963, The Grail. GIA Publications, Inc. North American agent.
All rights reserved. Used with permission.

13. Amazing Grace

Acc. p. 8

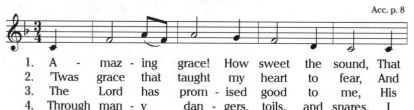

1. A - maz - ing grace! How sweet the sound, That
2. 'Twas grace that taught my heart to fear, And
3. The Lord has prom - ised good to me, His
4. Through man - y dan - gers, toils, and snares, I
5. When we've been there ten thou - sand years, Bright

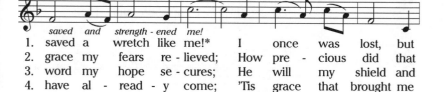

saved and strength - ened me!
1. saved a wretch like me!* I once was lost, but
2. grace my fears re - lieved; How pre - cious did that
3. word my hope se - cures; He will my shield and
4. have al - read - y come; 'Tis grace that brought me
5. shin - ing as the sun, We've no less days to

1. now am found, Was blind, but now I see.
2. grace ap - pear The hour I first be - lieved!
3. por - tion be As long as life en - dures.
4. safe thus far, And grace will lead me home.
5. sing God's praise Than when we'd first be - gun.

*This phrase has been restored to respect the author's original text. An alternate text is provided in *italic*.

Text: John Newton, 1725–1807, alt., vv. 1-4; John Rees, fl. 1859, v. 5.
Music: Early American Melody, 1831; adapt. Edwin Othello Excell, 1851–1921.

14. Be Not Afraid

Acc. p. 12

VERSE 1

1. You shall cross the bar-ren des-ert, but you shall not die of thirst. You shall wan-der far in safe-ty though you do not know the way. You shall speak your words in for-eign lands and all will un-der-stand. You shall see the face of God and live.

REFRAIN

Be not a-fraid. I go be-fore you al-ways. Come, fol-low me, and I will give you rest.

2. If you pass through raging waters in the sea, you shall not drown.
   If you walk amid the burning flames, you shall not be harmed.
   If you stand before the pow'r of hell and death is at your side,
   know that I am with you through it all.

3. Blessed are your poor, for the kingdom shall be theirs.
   Blest are you that weep and mourn, for one day you shall laugh.
   And if wicked tongues insult and hate you all because of me,
   blessed, blessed are you!

15. Because the Lord Is My Shepherd

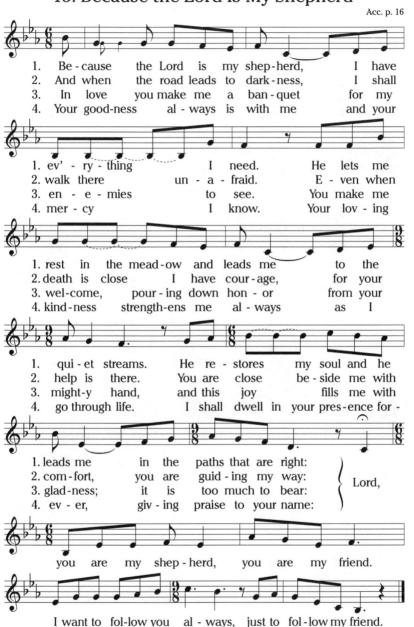

Acc. p. 16

16. Blest Are They

Acc. p. 18

1. Blest are they, the poor in spir - it, theirs is the
2. Blest are they, the low - ly ones,___ they shall in -
3. Blest are they___ who show mer - cy, mer___ - cy
4. Blest are they___ who seek peace;___ they are the
5. Blest are you who suf - fer hate,___ all___ be -

1. king - dom of God.___ Blest___ are they___
2. her - it the earth.___ Blest___ are they who
3. shall___ be theirs.___ Blest___ are they, the
4. chil - dren of God.___ Blest___ are they who
5. cause___ of me.___ Re - joice and be glad,___

1. full___ of sor - row, they___ shall be___ con - soled.
2. hun - ger and thirst,___ they___ shall have___ their fill.
3. pure___ of heart,___ they___ shall see God!
4. suf - fer in faith, the glo - ry of God___ is theirs.
5. yours is the king - dom; shine___ for all___ to see.

1.-5. Re - joice___ and be glad!___ Bless - ed are you,

ho - ly are you! Re - joice___ and be glad!___

Yours is the king - dom of God!___

17. Day Is Done

Acc. p. 38

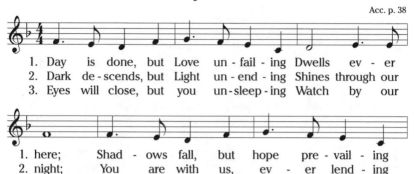

1. Day is done, but Love un - fail - ing Dwells ev - er
2. Dark de - scends, but Light un - end - ing Shines through our
3. Eyes will close, but you un - sleep - ing Watch by our

1. here; Shad - ows fall, but hope pre - vail - ing
2. night; You are with us, ev - er lend - ing
3. side; Death may come, in Love's safe keep - ing

1. Calms ev - 'ry fear. Lov - ing Fa - ther, none for - sak - ing,
2. New strength to sight: One in love, your truth con - fess - ing,
3. Still we a - bide. God of love, all e - vil quell - ing,

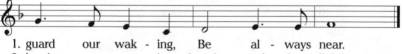

1. Take our hearts, of Love's own mak - ing, Watch our sleep - ing,
2. One in hope of heav - en's bless - ing, May we see, in
3. Sin for - giv - ing, fear dis - pell - ing, Stay with us, our

1. guard our wak - ing, Be al - ways near.
2. love's pos - sess - ing, Love's end - less light!
3. hearts in - dwell - ing, This e - ven - tide.

18. Enfold Me in Your Love

Acc. p. 42

1. You are the light that is e - ver bright,
2. You are the beau - ty that fills my soul,
3. You still the storms and the fear of night,
4. You are the word, full of life and truth,
5. You have re - stored me and par - doned sin,
6. You are the way, you are truth and life,

1. you fill my heart giv - ing life,
2. you by your wound make me whole,
3. you turn des - pair to de - light,
4. you guide my feet since my youth,
5. you give me strength from with - in,
6. you keep me safe in the strife.

1. you give the work I en - deav - or to do.
2. you paid the price to re - deem me from death;
3. you fill the an - guish and share in my tears,
4. you are my re - fuge, my firm cor - ner - stone;
5. you called me forth and my life you made new.
6. You give me love I can - not com - pre - hend,

1. Mean - ing and pur - pose are bless - ings from you.
2. yours is the love that sus - tains ev - 'ry breath.
3. you give me hope from the depths of my fears.
4. you I will wor - ship and hon - or a - lone.
5. Love is the bind - ing that holds me to you.
6. you guide the way to a life with - out end.

1.–6. O hold me, en - fold me in your love.

Text and music: Margaret Rizza, © 1998 Kevin Mayhew Ltd.
Administered and sub-published in North America by GIA Publications, Inc.

19. Eye Has Not Seen

Acc. p. 44

REFRAIN

Eye has not seen, ear has not heard what God has ready for those who love him; Spir-it of love, come, give us the mind of Je-sus, teach us the wis-dom of God.

To verses

VERSES

1. When pain and sor-row weigh us down, be near to us,
2. Our lives are but a sin-gle breath, we flow-er and
3. To those who see with eyes of faith, the Lord is ev-

1. O Lord, for-give the weak-ness of our faith, and
2. we fade, yet all our days are in your hands, so
3. er near, re-flect-ed in the fac - es, of

1. bear us up with-in your peace-ful word.
2. we re-turn in love what love has made.
3. all the poor and low-ly of the world.

4. We sing a mys-t'ry from the past in halls where saints have

4. trod, yet ev-er new the mu-sic rings to

4. Je-sus, Liv-ing Song of God.

20. God of Love

Acc. p. 48

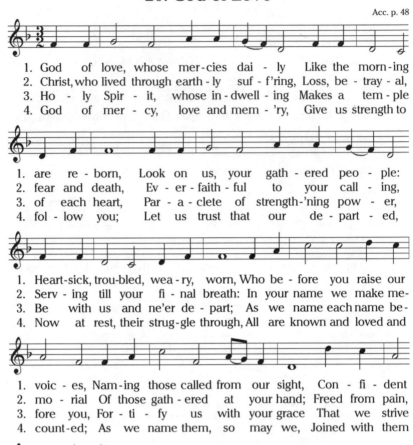

1. God of love, whose mer-cies dai - ly Like the morn-ing
2. Christ, who lived through earth - ly suf - f'ring, Loss, be - tray - al,
3. Ho - ly Spir - it, whose in - dwell - ing Makes a tem - ple
4. God of mer - cy, love and mem - 'ry, Give us strength to

1. are re - born, Look on us, your gath - ered peo - ple:
2. fear and death, Ev - er - faith - ful to your call - ing,
3. of each heart, Par - a - clete of strength-'ning pow - er,
4. fol - low you; Let us trust that our de - part - ed,

1. Heart-sick, trou-bled, wea - ry, worn, Who be - fore you raise our
2. Serv - ing till your fi - nal breath: In your name we make me-
3. Be with us and ne'er de - part; As we name each name be-
4. Now at rest, their strug-gle through, All are known and loved and

1. voic - es, Nam-ing those called from our sight, Con - fi - dent
2. mo - rial Of those gath - ered at your hand; Freed from pain,
3. fore you, For - ti - fy us with your grace That we strive
4. count-ed; As we name them, so may we, Joined with them

1. that each is pre - cious And is pres - ent in your light.
2. de - spair and sor - row, Ris - en Lord, with you they stand.
3. to live in whole-ness Till in heav'n we see your face.
4. in one com-mun - ion, Lov-ing, serv - ing, ev - er be.

Text: J. Michael Thompson, b. 1953, © 1994, World Library Publications, Inc.
All rights reserved. Used with permission.
Music: BEACH SPRING, 87 87 D; *The Sacred Harp*, Philadelphia, 1844.

21. Holy Darkness

Acc. p. 50

REFRAIN

Ho - ly dark-ness, bless-ed night, heav-en's an - swer hid-den from our sight. As we a - wait you, O God of si - lence, we em-brace your ho - ly night.

22. I Call You to My Father's House

Acc. p. 52

1. I call you to my Fa - ther's house, a
2. Lay down your sor - row, calm your fear; the
3. Al - though the way be hard and long in -
4. I have pre - pared a wed - ding feast of
5. I call you to my Fa - ther's house, a

1. love - ly dwell - ing place. He comes to meet you
2. Fa - ther bids you come. With o - pen arms he
3. to the prom - ised land, be not a - fraid to
4. fin - est food and wine. O join us at this
5. love - ly dwell - ing place. Be not a - fraid to

1. on the road, arms read - y to em - brace.
2. wel - comes you to your e - ter - nal home.
3. walk with me: I hold you by the hand.
4. ban - quet where my friends, the saints, now dine.
5. trav - el there and meet him face to face.

23. I Know That My Redeemer Lives

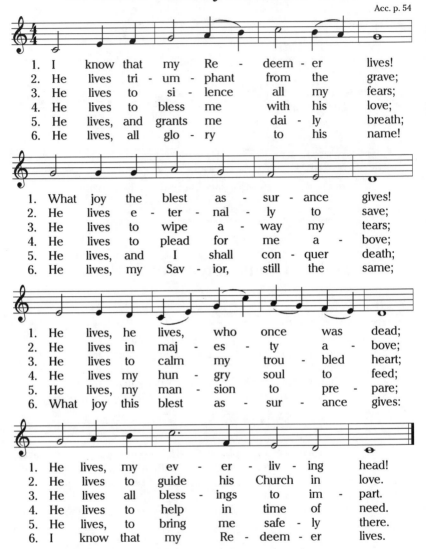

Acc. p. 54

1. I know that my Re - deem - er lives!
2. He lives tri - um - phant from the grave;
3. He lives to si - lence all my fears;
4. He lives to bless me with his love;
5. He lives, and grants me dai - ly breath;
6. He lives, all glo - ry to his name!

1. What joy the blest as - sur - ance gives!
2. He lives e - ter - nal - ly to save;
3. He lives to wipe a - way my tears;
4. He lives to plead for me a - bove;
5. He lives, and I shall con - quer death;
6. He lives, my Sav - ior, still the same;

1. He lives, he lives, who once was dead;
2. He lives in maj - es - ty a - bove;
3. He lives to calm my trou - bled heart;
4. He lives my hun - gry soul to feed;
5. He lives, my man - sion to pre - pare;
6. What joy this blest as - sur - ance gives:

1. He lives, my ev - er - liv - ing head!
2. He lives to guide his Church in love.
3. He lives all bless - ings to im - part.
4. He lives to help in time of need.
5. He lives, to bring me safe - ly there.
6. I know that my Re - deem - er lives.

Text: Samuel Medley, 1738–1799, alt.
Music: DUKE STREET, LM; John Hatton, ca. 1710–1793.

24. In the Lord Is My Joy

Acc. p. 59

In the Lord is my joy and sal-va-tion, he gives light

to all his cre-a-tion. In the Lord is my joy and sal-

va-tion, he gives peace and true con-so-la-tion.

25. Jerusalem, My Happy Home

Acc. p. 62

1. Je - ru - sa - lem, my hap - py home, When
2. O hap - py har - bor of the saints, O
3. Your gar - dens and your gal - lant walks Con -
4. There trees for - ev - er - more bear fruit And
5. Je - ru - sa - lem, Je - ru - sa - lem, God

1. shall I come to thee? When shall my sor - rows
2. sweet and pleas - ant soil! In you no sor - row
3. tin - ual - ly are green; There grow such sweet and
4. ev - er - more do spring; There ev - er - more the
5. grant that I may see Your end - less joy, and

1. have an end? Your joys when shall I see.
2. may be found, No grief, no care, no toil.
3. pleas - ant flow'rs As no - where else are seen.
4. an - gels sit And ev - er - more do sing!
5. of the same Par - tak - er ev - er be!

26. The King Shall Come

Acc. p. 188

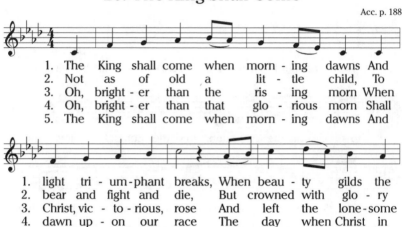

1. The King shall come when morn - ing dawns And
2. Not as of old a lit - tle child, To
3. Oh, bright - er than the ris - ing morn When
4. Oh, bright - er than that glo - rious morn Shall
5. The King shall come when morn - ing dawns And

1. light tri - um - phant breaks, When beau - ty gilds the
2. bear and fight and die, But crowned with glo - ry
3. Christ, vic - to - rious, rose And left the lone - some
4. dawn up - on our race The day when Christ in
5. light and beau - ty brings. Hail, Christ the Lord! Your

1. east - ern hills And life to joy a - wakes.
2. like the sun That lights the morn - ing sky.
3. place of death, De - spite the rage of foes.
4. splen - dor comes, And we shall see his face.
5. peo - ple pray: Come quick - ly, King of kings.

Text: John Brownlie, 1859–1925, alt. Music: MORNING SONG, CM, *Kentucky Harmony,* 1816.

27. Lord of All Hopefulness

Acc. p. 68

1. Lord of all hope - ful - ness, Lord of all joy, Whose
2. Lord of all ea - ger - ness, Lord of all faith, Whose
3. Lord of all kind - li - ness, Lord of all grace, Your
4. Lord of all gen - tle - ness, Lord of all calm, Whose

1. trust, ev - er child - like, no care could de - stroy:
2. strong hands were skilled at the plane and the lathe:
3. hands swift to wel - come, your arms to em - brace:
4. voice is con - tent - ment, whose pres - ence is balm:

1. Be there at our wak-ing, and give us, we pray, Your
2. Be there at our la-bors, and give us, we pray, Your
3. Be there at our hom-ing, and give us, we pray, Your
4. Be there at our sleep-ing, and give us, we pray, Your

1. bliss in our hearts, Lord, at the break of the day.
2. strength in our hearts, Lord, at the noon of the day.
3. love in our hearts, Lord, at the eve of the day.
4. peace in our hearts, Lord, at the end of the day.

28. Mary's Song

Acc. p. 70

1. My soul pro-claims the Lord my God. My
2. All na-tions now will share my joy; For
3. For those who fear the Ho-ly One, God's
4. God fills the hun-gry with good things; And
5. Then let all na-tions praise our God, The

1. Spir-it sings God's praise, Who looks on me,
2. gifts God has out-poured. This low-ly one
3. mer-cy will not die. Whose strong right arm
4. sends the rich a-way. The pro-mise made
5. Fa-ther and the Son, The Spir-it blest,

1. and lifts me up, That glad-ness fills my days.
2. has been made great. I mag-ni-fy the Lord.
3. puts down the proud, And lifts the low-ly high.
4. to A-bra-ham Is filled to end-less day.
5. who lives in us, While end-less a-ges run.

29. Lord of the Living

Acc. p. 69

1. Lord   of   the   liv - ing,   in   your   name   as - sem - bled,
2. Help   us   to   treas - ure   all   that   will   re - mind   us
3. May   we, when - ev - er   tempt - ed   to   de - jec - tion,
4. Lord,   you   can   lift   us   from   the   grave   of   sor - row

1. We   join   to   thank   you   for   the   life   re - mem - bered.
2. Of   the   en - rich - ment   in   the   days   be - hind   us.
3. Strong - ly   re - cap - ture   thoughts   of   res - ur - rec - tion.
4. In - to   the   pres - ence   of   your   own   to - mor - row:

1. Fa - ther,   have   mer - cy,   to   your   chil - dren   giv - ing
2. Your   love   has   set   us   in   the   gen - er - a - tions,
3. You   gave   us   Je - sus   to   de - feat   our   sad - ness
4. Give   to   your   peo - ple   for   the   day's   af - flic - tion

1. Hope   in   be - liev - ing.
2. God   of   cre - a - tion.
3. With   East - er   glad - ness.
4. Your   ben - e - dic - tion.

30. Now the Green Blade Rises

Acc. p. 92

1. Now the green blade ris - es from the bur - ied grain,
2. In the grave they laid him, love by ha - tred slain,
3. Forth he came at East - er, like the ris - en grain,
4. When our hearts are win - try, griev-ing or in pain,

1. Wheat that in dark earth man - y days has lain;
2. Think - ing that he would nev - er wake a - gain,
3. He that for three days in the grave had lain;
4. Your touch can call us back to life a - gain,

1. Love lives a - gain, that with the dead has been;
2. Laid in the earth like grain that sleeps un - seen;
3. Raised from the dead, my liv - ing Lord is seen;
4. Fields of our hearts that dead and bare have been;

1.-4. Love is come a - gain like wheat a - ris - ing green.

Text: John Macleod Campbell Crum, 1872–1958, © 1964, Oxford University Press.
Music: NOËL NOUVELET; trad. French carol.

31. On Eagle's Wings

Acc. p. 94

VERSE 1

1. You who dwell in the shel-ter of the Lord, who a-
bide in his shad-ow for life, say to the Lord: "My
ref-uge, my rock in whom I trust!"

REFRAIN

And he will raise you up on ea-gle's wings, bear you on the
breath of dawn, make you to shine like the sun, and
hold you in the palm of his hand.

2. The snare of the fowler will never capture you,
   and famine will bring you no fear:
   under his wings your refuge,
   his faithfulness your shield.

3. You need not fear the terror of the night,
   nor the arrow that flies by day;
   though thousands fall about you,
   near you it shall not come.

4. For to his angels he's given a command
   to guard you in all of your ways;
   upon their hands they will bear you up,
   lest you dash your foot against a stone.

32. Stand Firm in Faith

Acc. p. 184

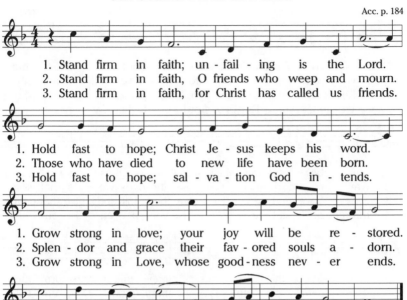

1. Stand firm in faith; un-fail-ing is the Lord.
2. Stand firm in faith, O friends who weep and mourn.
3. Stand firm in faith, for Christ has called us friends.

1. Hold fast to hope; Christ Je-sus keeps his word.
2. Those who have died to new life have been born.
3. Hold fast to hope; sal-va-tion God in-tends.

1. Grow strong in love; your joy will be re-stored.
2. Splen-dor and grace their fav-ored souls a-dorn.
3. Grow strong in Love, whose good-ness nev-er ends.

1. Life shall be yours, al-le-lu-ia!
2. Life shall be theirs, al-le-lu-ia!
3. Life shall be ours, al-le-lu-ia!

Music: SINE NOMINE 10 10 10 with alleluias, Ralph Vaughan Williams, 1872–1958.

33. We Offer Prayer in Sorrow, Lord

Acc. p. 189

1. We of-fer pray'r in sor-row, Lord, As-sist our
2. O com-fort us, we do be-lieve But find the
3. Re-ceive in-to your dwell-ing place All those whose
4. We praise you, Fa-ther, Lord of Light, We praise you

1. frail be-liev-ing. Make strong in us those pow'r-ful words
2. way so dark-ened. We miss the ones we do not see.
3. lives have end-ed. For-give their sins and give that peace
4. through our sad-ness. We praise you, ris-en Je-sus Christ,

1. To Mar-tha in her griev-ing: "Your bro-ther,
2. The pain of life is sharp-ened. O come with
3. For which they were in-tend-ed. You died, O
4. Who tri-umphed o-ver dark-ness. We praise you,

1. though now dead, will rise. For those who trust me
2. com-fort, gen-tle Word, Be close to us, for
3. Lord, that they might live, Have mer-cy, in your
4. Spir-it of them both, O come with glad-ness,

1. will not die." O hear these words of plead-ing.
2. in you, Lord, We find our own de-part-ed.
3. love for-give, For-give where they of-fend-ed.
4. give us hope, And mi-ti-gate death's harsh-ness.

34. We Thank You, Father, Lord of All

Acc. p. 190

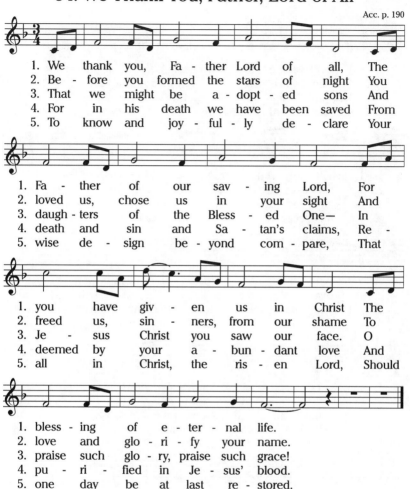

1. We thank you, Fa - ther Lord of all, The
2. Be - fore you formed the stars of night You
3. That we might be a - dopt - ed sons And
4. For in his death we have been saved From
5. To know and joy - ful - ly de - clare Your

1. Fa - ther of our sav - ing Lord, For
2. loved us, chose us in your sight And
3. daugh - ters of the Bless - ed One— In
4. death and sin and Sa - tan's claims, Re -
5. wise de - sign be - yond com - pare, That

1. you have giv - en us in Christ The
2. freed us, sin - ners, from our shame To
3. Je - sus Christ you saw our face. O
4. deemed by your a - bun - dant love And
5. all in Christ, the ris - en Lord, Should

1. bless - ing of e - ter - nal life.
2. love and glo - ri - fy your name.
3. praise such glo - ry, praise such grace!
4. pu - ri - fied in Je - sus' blood.
5. one day be at last re - stored.

Text: Ralph Wright, O.S.B., © 1984, St. Louis Abbey, St Louis, MO 63141. All rights reserved. Used with permission.
Music: PROSPECT, 88 88; William Walher's *Southern Harmony*.

35. You Are Mine

Acc. p. 196

VERSES

1. I will come to you in the si - lence,
2. I am hope for all who are hope-less,
3. I am strength for all the des - pair - ing,
4. am the Word that leads all to free - dom, I

1. I will lift you from____ all your fear.
2. I am eyes for all who long to see. In the
3. heal - ing for the ones who dwell in shame.
4. am the peace the world____ can - not give.

1. You will hear my voice, I claim you as my
2. shad - ows of the night,____ I will be your
3. All the blind will see, the lame will all run
4. I will call your name, em - brac - ing all your

1. choice, be still and know I am here. *(To verse 2)*
2. light,____ come and rest in me. *(To refrain)*
3. free, and all will know my name. *(To refrain)*
4. pain, stand up, now walk, and live! *(To refrain)*

REFRAIN

Do not be a - fraid, I am with you. I have called you

each by name. Come and fol - low me, I will bring you

home; I love you and you are mine. 4. I

36. Salmo 15: Protégeme, Dios Mío/ Psalm 16: Keep Me Safe, O God

Acc. p. 136

(Español) Pro - té - ge - me, Dios mí - o, pro -
(Bilingüe) Pro - té - ge - me, Dios mí - o, pro -

té - ge - me, Dios mí - o, que me re - fu - gio
té - ge - me, Dios mí - o. ⸮ Keep me safe,

en ti, me re - fu - gio en ti.
O God, ⸮ keep me safe, O God.

37. Salmo 18: Señor, Tú Tienes Palabras/ Psalm 19: Lord, You Have the Words

Acc. p. 138

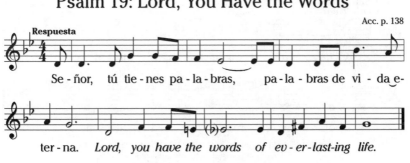

Respuesta

Se - ñor, tú tie - nes pa - la - bras, pa - la - bras de vi - da e -

ter - na. Lord, you have the words of ev - er - last - ing life.

38. Salmo 26: El Señor Es Mi Luz/
Psalm 27: The Lord Is My Light

Acc. p. 152

(Bilingual) El Se - ñor es mi luz   y mi sal - va - ción,
(Español) El Se - ñor es mi luz   y mi sal - va - ción,
(English) The Lord is my light___ and my sal - va - tion,

whom shall I fear?   Whom shall I
¿a quién te - me - ré?   ¿A quién te - me-
whom shall I fear?   Whom shall I

fear?   ¿A quién te - me - ré?
ré?   ¿A quién te - me - ré?
fear?   Whom shall I fear?

39. Salmo 62: Mi Alma Tiene Sed

ESTRIBILLO
Cantor/Todos

Acc. p. 159

Se - ñor,   mi al - ma tie - ne sed   de ti.

(Final)

Se - ñor,   mi al - ma tie - ne sed   de ti.

40. Salmo 83: Dichosos los que Viven

Acc. p. 162

Di - cho - sos   los que vi - ven   en tu ca - sa, Se - ñor.

Di - cho - sos   los que vi - ven   en tu ca - sa, Se - ñor.

41. Salmo 84: Muéstranos, Señor/ Psalm 85: Show Us, O Lord

RESPUESTA

Acc. p. 164

Mués-tra - nos, Se - ñor,   tu mi - se - ri - cor - dia   y
Show   us, O Lord,   your mer - cy and kind-ness and

da-nos tu sal - va - ción,   y da-nos tu sal - va - ción.
grant us your sal - va - tion, and grant us your sal - va - tion.

42. Salmo 102: El Señor es Compasivo/ Psalm 103: The Lord Is Rich In Kindness

ESTRIBILLO / REFRAIN

Todos/All

Acc. p. 168

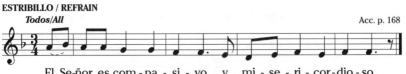

El Se-ñor es com - pa - si - vo y mi - se - ri - cor-dio - so.
The   Lord is rich in kind-ness, a-bound-ing in com-pas-sion.

43. Cerca Está el Señor/The Lord Is Near

Acc. p. 30

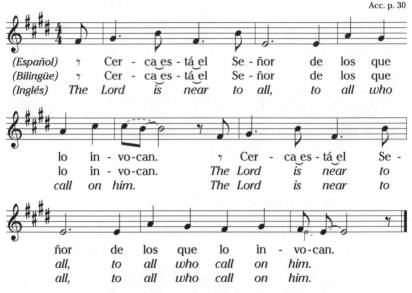

(Español) Cer - ca es - tá el Se - ñor de los que
(Bilingüe) Cer - ca es - tá el Se - ñor de los que
(Inglés) The Lord is near to all, to all who

lo in - vo-can. Cer - ca es - tá el Se -
lo in - vo-can. The Lord is near to
call on him. The Lord is near to

ñor de los que lo in - vo-can.
all, to all who call on him.
all, to all who call on him.

44. Cristo Vence

Acc. p. 35

ESTRIBILLO *Fin*

Cris-to ven-ce, Cris-to im-pe-ra. Cris-to, Cris-to rei - na-rá.

ESTROFAS

1. A - la - bad al Señor todas las na - cio - nes,
2. Pues reforzó su amor so - bre no - so - tros,
3. Gloria al Pa - dre y al Hi - jo
4. Como era en un principio, a - ho - ra y siem-pre

(al Estribillo)

1. ensalzadle to - das las gen - tes.
2. y la verdad del Señor es e - ter - na.
3. y al Es - pí - ri - tu San - to.
4. por los siglos de los si - glos, A - mén.

Text and music: Traditional.

45. Acuérdate de Jesucristo/Keep in Mind

Acc. p. 6

ESTRIBILLO

A - cuér - da - te de Je - su - cris - to re - su - ci - ta - do de en-tre los muer-tos. Él es nues-tra sal - va -

REFRAIN

Keep in mind that Je - sus Christ has died for us And is ris - en from the dead. He is our sav-ing Lord, He is joy for all a - ges.

ESTROFAS / VERSES *(Al Estribillo / To Refrain)*

1. Si con él mo - ri - mos, vi - vi - re - mos con él.
   Si con él su - fri - mos, rei - na - re - mos con él.

1. If we die with the Lord, we shall live with the Lord.
   If we en-dure with the Lord, we shall reign with the Lord.

(Al Estribillo / To Refrain)

2. En él nues-tras pe - nas, en él nues - tro go - zo.
   En él la es-pe - ran - za, en él nues-tro a - mor.
3. En él to - da gra - cia, en él nues - tra paz.
   En él nues-tra glo - ria, en él la sal - va - ción.

2. In Christ all our sor - row, in Christ all our joy.
   In him hope of glo - ry, in him all our love.
3. In Christ our re - demp-tion, in Christ all our grace.
   In him our sal - va - tion, in him all our peace.

Text and music: Lucian Deiss; Spanish trans.: María Pilar de la Figuera.

46. Arriba los Corazones

ESTRIBILLO

A - rri - ba   los   co - ra - zo - nes,   va - ya - mos

to - dos   al   pan   de   vi - da   que es fuen - te   de

glo-ria e-ter-na, de for - ta - le-za   y de a-le - grí - a.

ESTROFAS

1. A ti a - cu - di-mos se-dien - tos: Ven,   Se - ñor.
   Que - re - mos dar-te   la   vi - da: Ven,   Se - ñor;

2. Que - re - mos ser más her-ma - nos: Ven,   Se - ñor.
   En ti ha - lla - re-mos la fuer - za: Ven,   Se - ñor,

3. Que no ha-ya   lu-chas fra-ter - nas: Ven,   Se - ñor,
   A - par - ta el o - dio del mun - do: Ven,   Se - ñor,

1. Te - ne-mos fe en tu   mis-te - rio: Ven,   Se - ñor.
   con sus do - lo - res   y   di - chas: Ven,   Se - ñor. *(al Estribillo)*

2. Que nun - ca nos   ol - vi - da - mos: Ven,   Se - ñor.
   pa-ra ol - vi - dar las   o - fen - sas: Ven,   Se - ñor. *(al Estribillo)*

3. ni es-cla - vi - tud, ni   mi - se - rias: Ven,   Se - ñor.
   que ex-is - ta un or - den más jus - to: Ven,   Se - ñor. *(al Estribillo)*

Text and music: Traditional.

47. Quién Es Ese

Acc. p. 128

ESTROFAS

1. ¿Quién es e - se que ca - mi - na en las a - guas?
2. ¿Quién es e - se que los ma - res o - be - de - cen?
3. ¿Quién es e - se que_a no - so - tros ha lle - ga - do?

1. ¿Quién es e - se que_a los sor - dos ha - ce_o - ír?
2. ¿Quién es e - se que_a los mu - dos ha - ce_ha - blar?
3. ¿Quién es é - se, Sal - va - dor y Re - den - tor?

1. ¿Quién es e - se que_a los muer - tos re - su - ci - ta?
2. ¿Quién es e - se que da paz al al - ma_he - ri - da
3. ¿Quién es e - se que su_Es - pí - ri - tu nos de - ja

1. ¿Quién es e - se que su nom - bre quie - ro_o - ír?
2.   y pe - ca - dos con su muer - te per - do - nó?
3.   y trans - for - ma nues - tra vi - da con su_a - mor?

ESTRIBILLO

Es Je - sús, es Je - sús, Dios y

hom - bre que nos guí - a con su luz. luz.

Text and music: Traditional.

48. La Ruda Lucha Terminó/The Strife Is O'er

Acc. p. 65

ESTRIBILLO / REFRAIN

¡A - le - lu - ya, al - le - lu - ya, a - le - lu - ya!
Al - le - lu - ia, al - le - lu - ia, al - le - lu - ia!

ESTROFAS / VERSES

1. La ru - da lu - cha ter - mi - nó, la muer-te Cris - to con - quis-
1. *The strife is o'er, the bat - tle done; Now is the Vic-tor's tri - umph*

(al Estribillo / to Refrain)

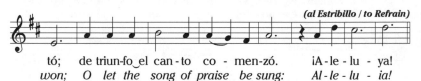

tó; de triun-fo el can - to co - men-zó. ¡A - le - lu - ya!
won; O let the song of praise be sung: Al - le - lu - ia!

2.
La muerte en Cristo se ensañó,
mas sus cadenas destrozó;
el Salvador resucitó.
¡Aleluya!

2.
Death's mightiest pow'rs have done their worst,
And Jesus has his foes dispersed;
Let shouts of praise and joy outburst:
Alleluia!

3.
Tres días fueron de dolor,
de luto por Cristo el Señor;
hoy vive y reina el Salvador.
¡Aleluya!

3.
He closed the yawning gates of hell;
The bars from heav'n's high portals fell;
Let hymns of praise his triumph tell:
Alleluia!

4.
Para librarnos del temor
de la cruel muerte y su terror
resucitó nuestro Señor.
¡Aleluya!

4.
On the third morn he rose again,
Glorious in majesty to reign;
O let us swell the joyful strain:
Alleluia!

English text by Francis Pott, 1832–1909, author of the Spanish text translation is anonymous.
Music: VICTORY; Giovanni da Palestrina, 1525–1594; adapt. by William H. Monk, 1823–1889.

49. Oye el Llamado

Acc. p. 97

ESTROFAS

1. Te - ne-bro-sas e - ran in - men-sas ti -
2. La vi - da sin Cris - to es u - na qui-
3. A - cép - ta-le_a Cris - to, Se - ñor de Se -

1. nie - blas; des-pre-cian la voz_____ de
2. me - ra; tan só-lo_es e - ter - na_____ en
3. ño - res; tam-bién Él pre-pa-ra_un_____ lu -

ESTRIBILLO

1. Cris - to_el Se - ñor.
2. Cris - to_el Se - ñor.
3. gar pa - ra ti.

O - ye_el lla - ma -

do. Te di - ce que vuel - vas. Él

quie-re lle-var - te por sen-da me - jor.

Text and music: Traditional.

50. Jesús, el Buen Pastor

Acc. p. 63

ESTRIBILLO

El Se-ñor es mi pas-tor, la vi-da ha da-do por mí; yo su voz he de_es-cu-char y su-yo siem-pre se-ré.

ESTROFAS

1. Yo___ soy el buen pas-tor;___ doy la vi-da_a mis o-ve - jas; por su nom-bre yo las lla-mo y con gran a-mor me si - guen.

2. Yo no soy el mer - ce - na - rio que_a-ban-do - na las o-ve - jas, cuan-do ve ve-nir al lo - bo, que las ma-ta_y las dis-per - sa.

3. Yo co-noz-co_a-mis o - ve - jas y_e - llas tam-bién me co-no - cen, co-mo_el Pa - dre me co-no-ce, yo tam-bién co-noz-co_al Pa - dre.

4. Ten-go_o-tras o - ve - jas le - jos y_es pre - ci - so que las trai - ga; mi lla - ma-da_es-cu-cha-rán___ y se_ha - rá só - lo_un re - ba - ño.

5. Mis o - ve - jas mi voz o - yen y me si - guen por do-quie - ra; yo les doy la vi-da_e - ter - na, e - llas no ve - rán la muer - te.

(al Estribillo)

51. La Muerte No Es el Final

Acc. p. 64

1. Tú nos di-jis-te que la muer-te no es el fi-nal del ca-
2. Cuan-do la pe-na nos al-can-za por un her-ma-no per-
3. Cuan-do, Se-ñor, re-su-ci-tas-te, to-dos ven-ci-mos con-

1. mi-no, que aun-que mo-ri-mos no so-mos
2. di-do, cuan-do el a-diós do-lo-ri-do
3. ti-go. Nos re-ga-las-te la vi-da

1. car-ne de un cie-go des-ti-no. Tú nos hi-cis-te. Tu-yos
2. bus-ca en la fe su es-pe-ran-za, en tu pa-la-bra con-fi-
3. co-mo en Be-ta-nia al a-mi-go. Si ca-mi-na-mos a tu

1. so-mos. Nues-tro des-ti-no es vi-vir sien-do fe-
2. a-mos, con la cer-te-za que Tú ya le has de-
3. la-do no va a fal-tar-nos tu a-mor, por-que mu-

1. li-ces con-ti-go, sin pa-de-cer ni mo-rir.
2. vuel-to a la vi-da, ya le has lle-va-do a la luz.
3. rien-do vi-vi-mos vi-da más cla-ra y me-jor.

52. Dale el Descanso, Señor

Acc. p. 36

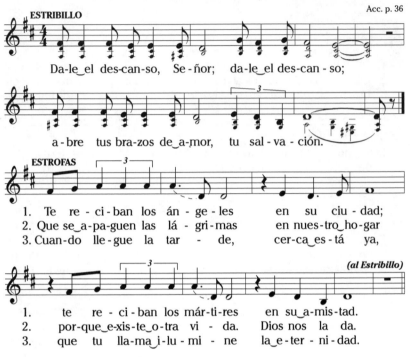

ESTRIBILLO

Da-le_el des-can-so, Se-ñor; da-le_el des-can - so;

a - bre tus bra-zos de_a-mor, tu sal - va - ción.

ESTROFAS

1. Te re - ci - ban los án - ge - les en su ciu - dad;
2. Que se_a-pa-guen las lá - gri-mas en nues-tro_ho-gar
3. Cuan-do lle - gue la tar - de, cer-ca_es - tá ya,

(al Estribillo)

1. te re - ci - ban los már-ti-res en su_a-mis-tad.
2. por-que_e-xis-te_o-tra vi - da. Dios nos la da.
3. que tu lla-ma_i-lu - mi - ne la_e - ter - ni - dad.

53. Canto de María

Acc. p. 27

ESTRIBILLO
Todos

Pro - cla-ma mi al-ma lo gran-de que_es Dios, se_a - le - gra mi_es-

1.   **2.**   *(A las Estrofas)*
    (Final)

pí - ri-tu_en mi sal - va-dor. Pro - mi sal-va - dor.

54. Las Puertas de la Nueva Ciudad

Acc. p. 66

ESTRIBILLO

Las puer-tas de la nue-va ciu-dad se a-bren pa-ra ti.

Las puer-tas de la nue-va ciu-dad se a-bren pa-ra ti.

Y Dios tu a-mi - go, te sal-va - rá, te sal-va - rá.

ESTROFAS

1. Ve - rás el nue-vo dí - a, el nue-vo Sol; ve -
2. Ve - ni-mos en fa-mi - lia jun-to al al - tar; el

1. rás la nue-va vi - da, Re - su - rrec - ción; la
2. pan que re - su-ci - ta Dios nos lo da; el

(al Estribillo)

1. gran no-ti - cia: Dios es a - mor, Dios es a - mor.
2. pan de vi - da nos man-ten-drá en su a-mis-tad.

INDEX/ÍNDICE

* indicates the piece may be sung bilingually

Hymn No.

45   *Acuérdate de Jesucristo
13   Amazing Grace
46   Arriba los Corazones
14   Be Not Afraid
15   Because the Lord Is My Shepherd
16   Blest Are They
     Canticle of Mary (pg. 28)
     Canticle of Philippians (pg. 24)
     Cántico de Filipenses (pg. 25)
     Cántico de Mariá (pg. 29)
53   Canto de María
43   *Cerca Está el Señor
44   Cristo Vence
52   Dale el Descanso, Señor
17   Day Is Done
18   Enfold Me in Your Love
19   Eye Has Not Seen
20   God of Love
21   Holy Darkness
22   I Call You to My Father's House
23   I Know that My Redeemer Lives
24   In the Lord Is My Joy
25   Jerusalem, My Happy Home
50   Jesús, el Buen Pastor
45   *Keep In Mind
51   La Muerte No Es el Final
48   *La Ruda Lucha Terminó
54   Las Puertas de la Nueva Ciudad
27   Lord of All Hopefulness
29   Lord of the Living
28   Mary's Song
30   Now the Green Blade Rises
31   On Eagle's Wings
49   Oye el Llamado
36   *Psalm 16: Keep Me Safe, O God
1   Psalm 16: Shelter Me, O God
37   *Psalm 19: Lord, You Have the Words
2   Psalm 23: Shepherd Me, O God
3   Psalm 23: The Lord Is My Shepherd
4   Psalm 27: The Lord Is My Light (Haas)

Hymn No.

5   Psalm 27: The Lord Is My Light (Willcock)
38   *Psalm 27: The Lord Is My Light (Hurd)
7   Psalm 34: The Cry of the Poor
9   Psalm 42: Like the Deer That Yearns
6   Psalm 42/43: Like the Deer That Longs
8   Psalm 63: My Soul Is Thirsting
10   Psalm 63: Your Love Is Finer Than Life
12   Psalm 84: How Lovely Is Your Dwelling
     Place
41   *Psalm 85: Show Us, O Lord
42   *Psalm 103: The Lord Is Rich in Kindness
     Psalm 121: Our Help Comes from the
     Lord (pg. 20)
     Psalm 130: If You Kept a Record of Our
     Sins, O Lord (pg. 22)
11   Psalm 139: You Are Near
47   Quién Es Ese
36   *Salmo 15: Protégeme, Dios Mío
37   *Salmo 18: Señor, Tú Tienes Palabras
38   *Salmo 26: El Señor Es Mi Luz
39   Salmo 62: Mi Alma Tiene Sed
40   Salmo 83: Dichosos los que Viven
41   *Salmo 84: Muéstranos, Señor
42   *Salmo 102: El Señor es Compasivo
     Salmo 120: El Auxilio me Viene del Señor
     (pg. 21)
     Salmo 129: Si Llevas Cuenta de los
     Delitos (pg. 23)
1   Shelter Me, O God
2   Shepherd Me, O God
32   Stand Firm in Faith
7   The Cry of the Poor
26   The King Shall Come
43   *The Lord Is Near
48   *The Strife Is O'er
33   We Offer Prayer in Sorrow, Lord
34   We Thank You, Father, Lord of All
35   You Are Mine
11   You Are Near